WHAT'S HAPPENING TO OUR WORLD?

The Old Order Is Collapsing

ERNIE HASLER

authorHOUSE®

AuthorHouse™ UK
1663 Liberty Drive
Bloomington, IN 47403 USA
www.authorhouse.co.uk
Phone: 0800.197.4150

Published by AuthorHouse 07/19/2018

ISBN: 978-1-5462-9491-7 (sc)
ISBN: 978-1-5462-9490-0 (hc)
ISBN: 978-1-5462-9492-4 (e)

Print information available on the last page.

INTRODUCTION

We are in the Biblical "End Times" The Tribulation, encompasses a seven-year period when Yahweh (God) will discipline Israel and make a final judgment upon the false church members of the world.

This is called "The time of Jacobs trouble" read in your own bibles Jeremiah 30:4-7, Daniel 12:1,

I ask you to read these scriptures in your own Bibles to keep this booklet short and concise, so that readers will not get tired.

Note: I use the original Names Yahweh and Yeshua.

TODAY 2018?

As you watch the Brexit debacle in the Westminster Parliament, do you not wonder if the British Government has lost its marbles?

At its height of Empire, it was said: "That the sun did not set on the British peoples and Our Colonial Peoples".

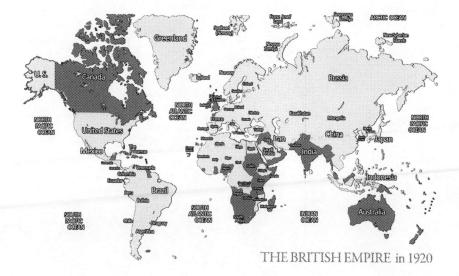

THE BRITISH EMPIRE in 1920

Due to the financial drain of two World Wars on Great Britain, the Americans took over as the most powerful nation on earth.

How did this fall in wealth and power come about?

The "Lost Tribes of Israel" having lost knowledge of our true identities and now thinking we are Gentiles. - Found ourselves benefactors of promises made to Abraham making us the richest and most powerful nations on earth and with such power and self-pride, we were less willing to yield to our Yahweh (God) and His ways.

We believed it was our own genius that made us superior and dominant to other nations.

Just like we see in the vote to leave the European Union, insulting all the highly talented incomer people working here, but, who are now leaving our arrogant nation in disgust, offended by our vain superiority.

It may surprise most of us, that this is all forecast in the Hebrew Bible. I have to warn you that modern bibles have had more than 6,000 instances of Yahweh's Name removed and replaced with Lord (Baal in English) or god what a huge deception.

After Yahweh had withheld the birthright 2520 years, (Yahweh is saying in Lev. 26, that if the Israelites forsook Yahweh, He would punish them by withholding the birthright for 2,520 years!) and then, when our peoples deserved nothing from Him, He suddenly bestowed on us national blessings unparalleled in history—the unconditional promise made to Abraham was kept! Amazing!

But! No longer is Yahweh obligated by His promise to continue our undeserving peoples in world prestige, wealth and greatness.

The Ten Commandments

1. You shall have no other Elohim's (gods) before Me.
2. You shall not make idols.
3. You shall not take Yahweh the name of your God in vain.
4. Remember the Sabbath day, to keep it holy.
5. Honor your father and your mother.
6. You shall not murder.
7. You shall not commit adultery.
8. You shall not steal.
9. You shall not bear false witness against your neighbor.
10. You shall not covet.

Once we had been given such unrivaled position, it was up to us whether we should keep it or reject Him.

But if we ignored Yahweh and His commandments, He warned that, He would break the "Pride of our Power".

Note these are shortened versions of the commandments. Read Exodus chapter 20 in your own bibles and note which day is Yahweh's Sabbath.

Instead of being ethical and honorable as Yahweh advised in the first five books of the Bible, the British leaders and people in positions of power have become self-opinionated liars and cheats.

Read Leviticus 26 to get the full picture. It basically promises blessings for obedience or punishments for disobedience.

The disastrous Brexit negations are going to suddenly drop Britain to the second division in world power and wealth and such is our nearly two trillion pounds international debt, we will be bankrupt, and our poorest people could end up eating grass.

Wake up: Bankruptcy is an imminent and real threat to once Great Britain.

The negative economic effect will also be felt across the world particularly in what remains of Europe.

Bible prophecy also tells us that America will also fall from world power, although it does not tell exactly how that happens. Although Donald Trump seems to be making a thorough job of isolating the world's once great and leading nation.

His isolationist polices has already elevated China to the most influential nation on our planet.

His continued persecution of all non-white Americans could lead to civil war.

Who knows, only time will tell, but America will fall.

As proof of bible prophecy coming true read Isaiah 17:1 An amazing prophecy against Damascus.

This reflects the beginning of an invasion and final destruction of Damascus as prophesied in the Bible Read Isaiah 17: Verse 1, and Amos 1, where He is speaking of Syria and Bashar al-Assad President of Syria.

BUT THE WORLD CRISES ARE NOT OVER.

We can see the world is in crisis now with economic troubles, crime, uprisings, riots, wars, earthquakes, hurricanes, typhoons, flooding, volcanos erupting, terrorism, forest fires and famine.

But there is yet another huge crisis due to hit the world. Read Revelations 8:7

We can see forest and grass fires happening on our television screens today, but still we burn vast quantities of carbon fuel continuing the increase in world temperatures.

Worse still, vast quantities of methane gas are being released by melting permafrost in artic regions, accelerating global warming.

Forests and grain farmlands are now at serious risk from uncontrollable fires, and these are the real game changer.

The reality is that global warming is in a positive feed back loop, we have passed the point of no return. Global temperature will continue to rise and the weather disasters we see on our television screens will get even worse.

This crisis to come upon the world will be the catalyst for all the world governments when they reach a state of despair, to call on the perceived important religious leader and his political partner, to establish strict discipline on all the world and bring on a mark as proof of everyone compliance with his churches orders.

Those who don't accept the mark or membership of this world church will not be able to buy or sell.

It is join the church or starve.

Forest fires and grain crop fires are soon to become frightening and beyond the control of governments and all their military forces.

Along with global warming sea levels are rapidly rising and land areas are already at risk.

WAR AGAINST ISRAEL IS IMMINENT.

Iranian supreme leader Ayatollah Ali Khamenei and a map of the Middle East.

Land road from Tehran across Iraq and Syria to the Mediterranean cause for his feast.

A case of seizing opportunity out of chaos; since 2014, building a road under noses.

Of enemies engaged in the terrible slaughter, oblivious to the threat he poses.

Yes, his long-term aim of attacking Israel begins to materialize.

While the world, preoccupied in short-term crises, fails to realize

His aim is to move people and supplies to the Golan Heights,

Where he will establish his long-range artillery and rocket sites.

Yahweh (God) anciently warned that Iran (Persia), with Russia (Magog) and a coalition of allies (including Turkey, Libya, Sudan) will invade Israel in a huge act of war.

Poor little Israel must stand alone like in days of old, their faith—as usual—shaky, depending on Yahweh. For the United States will be unwilling (or unable) to help Israel defend herself anymore.

Then Iran, backed by Russia, Syria, Turkey, Libya, and Sudan invades; the future looks very, very black.

When things look bleak, divine intervention; is that thunder I hear, crack, crack, crack?

(Explanatory note about America: Just like the unbelievable demise of Great Britain is occurring before our eyes through Brexit, so America will also crash and will not be able to fix it or help Israel.)

WORLD LEADERS ADMIT DEFEAT.

Revelation 17 describes a powerful religious leader who deceives the entire world into following him. Read it in your own Bibles.

So, the leaders of this world will unite and give their power and support to this religious leader and his political partner.

Then the world will be in a position ready to enforce the mark of the beast and make almost everyone comply.

NOTE: The call for world unity and 'peace' is growing all the time because of all the troubles in the world.

Especially Climate Change which now is causing major weather disasters and has an unstoppable momentum.

The Christian Church is already calling for Sunday to be made sacred and justified as a carbon saving strategy.

Diaries and calendars have for several decades already been changed to start on a Monday, thereby making The Ba'al Day, Sunday, the seventh day of the week.

Many people are now not sure what is the true seventh day. (sneaky but deadly serious, as it could cause people to join the Beast Power thinking Sunday was the Sabbath.).

ENFORCED BY LAW

Now this is a major Bible prophecy end time event to be fulfilled. Read Revelation 13 in your own Bible.

Because of all the turmoil in the world, the church leaders, and the governments will unite in convincing the world that the mark of the beast will be the "solution" to the world's problems.

Of course, they will give it a more positive name.

They will convince the world (through deception) that all these troubles are the judgments of God because of us not keeping His law (what they mean is their law, Sunday, Christmas, Easter etc.).

And this is starting to happen already. Leaders in America have started attributing the disasters that are happening as God's judgments upon the world.

Now, the "remedy" that they propose and enforce will go against God's ten commandments. – One of which will be the enforcement of a Sunday Law.

The sad thing is, while the majority of the world are waiting for a physical mark of the beast to be enforced,

like a microchip or tattoo, the REAL mark will be a spiritual one and only God's true end time saints will be able to identify it, and the majority of the world will be deceived into taking it. For example, The Sabbath Day that one keeps.

This goes along with the law, only those with the Mark of the Beast can buy or sell.

Those who won't take the mark face starvation.

FINAL MESSAGE TO THE WORLD

Before anyone chooses for or against the mark of the beast.

Yahweh will send a final message to the world. This message is contained in the three angel's messages of Revelation 14 is Yahweh's last call of mercy to the world. Read Revelation 14 in your own Bibles.

Yahweh will give power to this final message to the world with His Holy Spirit, and many hearts will be convicted of the truth and will come out of Babylon.

Choose

In this end times timeline of final events, this is the most important time for every man, woman and child on earth.

We will all at this time have to make one final choice.

A choice to take the side of our brother Messiah Yeshua and receive the seal of Yahweh (Revelation 7:1-3; 14:1)

Or, under economic pressure and fear of persecution from the world, take the mark of the beast (Revelation 13:16).

Then we will have a world with only two groups of people. Those with the mark (who will be forever lost) and those witnesses with Yahweh's Seal (who will inherit eternal life).

The Seal of Yahweh - Exodus 31:16-17 ...'Wherefore the children of Israel shall keep the Sabbath, to observe the Sabbath throughout their generations, for a perpetual covenant.

It is a sign between me and the children of Israel for ever: for in six days Yahweh made heaven and earth, and on the seventh day he rested, and was refreshed.'

SALVATION WITHDRAWN

Once everyone has made their decision for the mark of the beast or the seal of Yahweh, then the door of mercy will close, and everyone will be judged either righteous or filthy ...

Read Revelation 22:11 in your own Bible.

So now at this point, there will be no more opportunities to be saved.

If you are lost, you remain lost, and if you are saved, you remain saved.

So, will it be at the end of this world, when Yahweh's mercy will finally come to an end for those who choose not to turn to Him.

Who will receive your allegiance? The beast system (Babylon), or Yahweh our Heavenly Father?

A Time of Trouble for Yahweh's People: - Daniel 12:1

When "Michael" stands up, as described in Daniel, the door of mercy is forever closed.

At this same time, the Spirit of Yahweh will be withdrawn from the earth and the world will be plunged into great spiritual darkness, with Satan using all His evil ways against the saints of Yahweh, unleashing his full fury upon them ...

Revelation 12:17 Read in your own Bible

This time is also mentioned in *Revelation 13:15* ...

This is a time when many of Yahweh's people who have rejected the mark of the beast will flee into the mountains to escape the persecution placed upon them by the enemy.

Satan will seek out Yahweh's people to kill them. But as it says in Daniel above, we need not fear because we shall be delivered!

We need to be thinking and asking Yahweh how we can escape to the hills, when this Satanic fever overwhelms people, they will become obsessed with identifying True Sabbath keepers and delivering them over to the forces of Babylon to be killed.

Remember this is not the first time, in the early centuries of the Christian church, between fifty and one hundred million True Sabbath keepers were hunted down and killed. Something similar is to be repeated at the end times.

It should also be realized that the Nazis did not come from some other planet. Those ordinary humans who did such fiendishly cruel things to Sabbath keepers (Jews) were themselves often Sunday church attending pillars of the Christian community.

Such is the power of propaganda and tribalism.

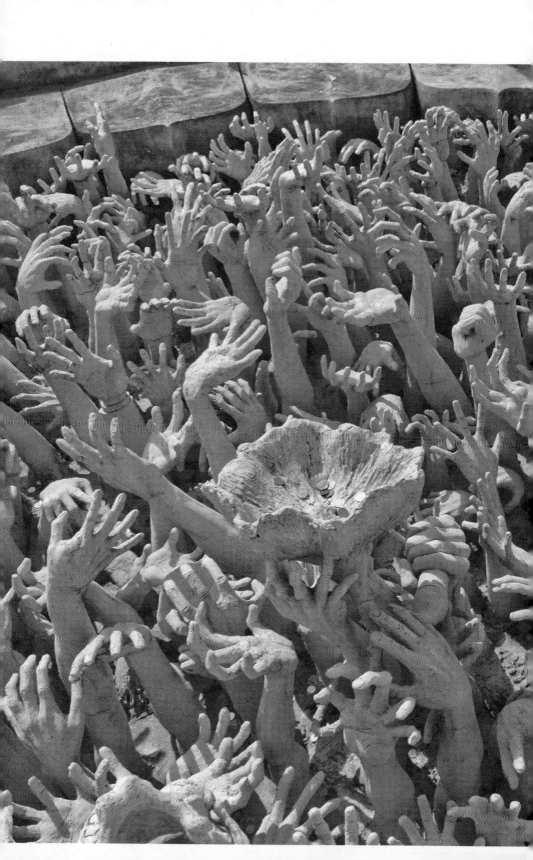

THE SEVEN LAST PLAGUES OF REVELATIONS

Now that everyone has decided to follow Messiah Yeshua and love Yahweh and all His commandments including all other people, or the beast and its apparent power.

Yahweh's final judgments can begin to fall upon this world, in the form of the seven last plagues. These plagues will be the as mentioned in Revelation 14:10. Read them in your own Bibles

In other words, those who receive the mark of the beast will receive the FULL wrath of Yahweh, and there will be no mercy "mixed in" with His judgments (plagues).

Now these plagues ONLY fall upon the lost. They only fall upon those who have disobeyed Yahweh's commandments and received the mark of the beast.

They will not come near those who have the seal of Yahweh (Seventh day Sabbath keepers and incidentally

the festivals of Yahweh as specified in Leviticus 23), as Yahweh's people will be fully protected, just like the Israelites were during the Ten Plagues in Egypt.

Read Leviticus 23 in your own Bible – It is so important.

THE GREAT BATTLE

This end time's event is the decisive battle between good and evil.

This is the worldwide spiritual battle between Satan's forces and Yahweh's people.

The battle of Armageddon is the climax of the spiritual war that has been raging between Yahweh and Satan since the beginning.

Sometime during this great battle, now Proxy (Just like Joseph was Proxy King of Egypt) Proxy King Yeshua returns as *"KING OF KINGS AND LORD OF LORDS"* to defeat Satan and his hosts and to deliver the saints.

I described this as the decisive battle, it will be desperate and terrible, as all the world forces throw themselves against King Yeshua and the impending Kingdom of Yahweh.

Note: - The Sign of the Son of Man was seen in the heavenly scroll on 23 September 2017 indicating His return as Trumpets 2020.

The Second Coming of Yeshua, the Messiah, now King Yeshua

The second coming of Yeshua will be a glorious, visible, fiery event that will make all other end time events look ordinary!

Accompanied by billions of mighty angels, King Yeshua will return in great glory to deliver His people.

There will be no rapture like so many believe, as the Bible clearly states that every eye will see Yeshua return, and that His second coming will be a noisy, fiery event.

Read Matthew 24:27; in your own Bible

Read 1 Thess. 4:16-17; in your own Bible

Read Matthew 24:42 -51; in your own Bible

Read Matthew Revelation 1:7; in your own Bible

Read 2 Peter 3:10. in your own Bible

Matthew 13:24-30 Read in your own Bible (There is no Rapture for the wheat in this explanation).

Matthew 13:38-40 ...Read this continuation of the above in your own bible.

THE RESURRECTION OF THE FAITHFUL

When Proxy King Yeshua returns at the second coming, the graves will burst open and the righteous will rise up with immortal bodies. And together with the saints who have gone through the great tribulation and are still alive, will meet King Yeshua in the air ...

1 Thessalonians 4:16-17 ...Read this in your own Bibles...

Revelation 20:5 ...The rest of the dead (lost) will not live again until the 1000 years are over. Read this in your own Bibles.

New Beginning

The fire that Yahweh reigns down upon the wicked has a dual purpose. First it destroys the wicked, included Satan himself. Secondly Yahweh uses it to cleanse and renew the earth.

In Noah's day the earth was cleansed and renewed with water. This time the earth is going to be renewed with fire ... *Revelation 21:1* ... Read this in your own Bibles. '– So, the earth is made new and the saints live for eternity with Brother Yeshua! And sin is no more!

Praise Yahweh! For His glorious plan.

These are the end times events. These are the Bible prophecy events to be fulfilled.

We are witnessing Isaiah 17 1 Right now on our television screens Read Isaiah 17:1 in your own Bibles.

We are also witnessing the demise of our arrogant nation Britain in shambolic Brexit negations.

Once the mark of the beast is enforced, we will know that we are living in the very last days, just before the second

coming of Brother Yeshua and the end of the world as we know it.

We need to humble ourselves now and return to Yahweh and His Sabbaths and just rest quietly in His presence listening to/for His silent Holy Spirit.

Hear Oh! Israel! Yahweh our Elohim is One and is the only Elohim.

BEGINNINGS
OF RELIGION

Written history (the age of formal writing) is only c.5000 years old.

But religion is much older.

Sun Worship - Baal, Alternative Titles: Baal Shamen, Baal Shemin, Baalim -god worshipped in many ancient Middle Eastern communities, especially among the Canaanites, who considered him one of the most important gods in the pantheon.

As a Semitic common noun *baal* (Hebrew *baʿal*) meant "owner" or "lord,". As such, Baal designated the universal god of fertility, and in that capacity his title was Prince, Lord of the Earth.

He was also called the Lord of Rain and Dew, the two forms of moisture that were indispensable for fertile soil in Canaan.

In Ugaritic and Hebrew, Baal's epithet as the storm god was He Who Rides on the Clouds. In Phoenician he was called Baal Shamen, Lord of the Heavens.

The sun was and still is, so important to the four seasons and all life on our planet, so it is understandable that to early humans the sun was considered a god. Not only a god, but the principal god.

Egypt, Assyria, Babylon, Meads and Persia, Greece and Rome, were the "world civilizations" of the old world-and the Aztecs, Incas, Mayas, Toltec culture and Sioux of the new world all, all worshiped the SUN!

The Christian Church continues this to this day with it's main Christmas Festival on the day the return of the sun which can be clearly discerned by lengthened day light on 25 December.

That was also the main purpose of the stone circles in the northern hemisphere, to predict the annual solar cycles.

The prophet Jeremiah tells us that the kings of Judah loved and served the sun and worshiped it (Jer 8:2).

Ezekiel provides a very graphic picture of sun worshipers in the Lord's house, facing East in worship of the sun (Ezek 8:16). Read it in your own Bible.

This is common in Christian churches on the morning sunrise services of their other principal festival Easter.

Promoted by the Christian Church as a "Christian" holiday, Easter celebrations date back into remotest antiquity and

are found around the world, as the blossoming of spring did not escape the notice of the ancients, who revered this life-renewing time of the year, when winter had completely passed, and the sun and the growing season was "born again.

Hence the fertility symbols of bunny rabbits and Easter eggs.

THE STATE
OF ISRAEL

The second defining Jewish event of the century was the achievement of the Zionist movement in the creation of the State of Israel in 1948.

Something that most people did not think was possible.

There had been strong and paramilitary opposition to British colonial rule for many years, and in 1947 the United Nations agreed a plan to partition the land between Jews and Arabs. In May 1948 the British Government withdrew their forces.

Immediately, the surrounding Arab States invaded, and the new Jewish State was forced to fight the first of several major wars.

Notable among these were the 6-day war in 1967 and the Yom Kippur war in 1973. When Israel was not military equipped to fight against such superior forces

The first steps towards a permanent peace came when Israel signed a peace treaty with Egypt in 1979, and with Jordan in 1994.

For most of its history Israel has had an uneasy relationship with the Arab states that surround it and has been greatly sustained by the help and support of the USA, where the Jewish community is large and influential.

The 21st century began with great political uncertainty over Israel and its relationship with the Palestinian people, and this continues to this day.

The beliefs of the original Jewish followers of Yeshua were Jewish;

Yeshua was the Messiah who they expected would return and rout the Romans to establish the Kingdom of Israel, but instead he was beaten, scourged and hung on a tree to die. A big disappointment.

However, those appealing to the pagans and god fearers (non-Jews who worshiped with the Jews) to try to save and grow their church, had to make some changes in their presentation of Yeshua for non-Jewish hearers.

The ancient worship of Mithra was even more widely accepted than Yahweh, Moses' Elohim.

Mirthra was known, in various forms, in India, Persia, Greece, and throughout the Roman Empire.

But Yeshua and Mithras had something important in common.

The promise to entice them to convert was eternal life in Yeshua's Kingdom of Elohim.

So, the successors to the original disciples incorporated Mithrasim into their story.

The True Teachings and Example of our human brother Messiah Yeshua.

The Nazarene Rabbi.

There was a wandering Jewish Rabbi supported by disciples both male and female who taught people to love Yahweh the only self-existent One and to love other people as themselves.

His name was Yeshua which means Yahweh's salvation.

He gathered a great following and publicly criticized the High priests for commercializing the temple, rituals.

For that he was falsely accused of lack of respect of the Roman Emperor and he was scourged and hung on a tree to die.

After death he was resurrected and appeared to over five hundred witnesses.

He promised to return, once the time of the gentiles was ended, as Yahweh's proxy King to establish His Kingdom and Torah rule over all the earth.

The sign of the son of man appeared in the stars on 23rd September 2017 indicating three years until his return. On Feast of Trumpets 2020.

There is still time to give Yahweh your allegiance, but only just enough time.

Model Yeshua's Teachings So People Are Drawn to Spirituality

Matthew 5:13-16 read these verses in your own Bible.

Listen for the "Oh! So silent, Holy Spirit speaking to You."

Author's comments: If you do not believe in Yahweh, if you are not prepared to reject all other gods and you are not prepared to welcome Him into your home or where ever you find yourself on His Sabbaths, you cannot expect His Holy Spirit will prompt or affect you.

It is not going to church or asking your minister or priest, who may be nice and charismatic people, but teach you to worship false gods and idols.

Yahweh the only true Elohim wants your personal company on his commanded assemblies (keeping His Sabbaths, you are part of His whole assembly even if you think you are alone).

Keeping His Sabbaths is: "The Sign that you belong to Yahweh". Yes, keeping His Sabbaths will mark you out, other people notice.

His Sabbaths start at Sunset and finish 24 hours later at Sunset.

The weekly Sabbath is the Seventh Day. Not Sunday.

High Sabbaths are on specific dates on the Hebrew Calendar, as listed in Leviticus 23, a bit confusing but not impossible to determine.

Keeping a Sabbath begins with lighting two Sabbath Candles, one reminds us to; Keep Yahweh's Sabbaths. The other reminds us to; Protect Yahweh's Sabbaths.

Usually, married women light two or more candles whilst some single women light just one candle. If no women are present, a man can light the Shabbat candles.

The candles should be lit in the room where the Friday night meal will be eaten.

After the candles are lit, the women cover their eyes and make the blessing.

Blessed are You, Yahweh our Elohim, King of the Universe, who has sanctified us with Your commandments, and commanded us to kindle the light of the holy Shabbat.

Note: There is no command in the Bible to light Sabbath Candles, but we are commanded to Keep Yahweh's Sabbaths and to Protect Yahweh's Sabbaths. That's what the two candles remind us to do.

Once you have made the blessing, you are ready to look up and enjoy the beauty of the candles.

Author's note: I have lung problems, so I had to stop burning real candles as the fumes made me choke, so I use battery powered LED imitation candles.

It is good to welcome Yahweh to be with you, in your home or where ever. Along the rough lines of:

Great Eternal Yahweh, I come before you in the name of my brother Yeshua, who willingly suffered and died to pay for my sins and selfishness, with his spilt blood to reconcile me with You.

I come before you to keep your Sabbath with You and I ask you to let your Holy Spirit guide, lead and correct me.

I declare, Hear OH! Israel, Yahweh our creator Elohim is One and is the only Elohim.

Shabbat Shalom.

You do not have to do anything or jump through hoops. Just rest in Yahweh's presence, even have a nap, try to be a blessing to family members, if suitable visit someone in hospital or even in jail.

Yahweh just wants you to accept Him and rest in His silent and invisible presence, in His Sabbaths.

You won't enjoy His Sabbaths until you lose the idea that you are keeping (working) His Sabbaths, when you learn to just rest (yes, even sleep) in His presence, you will find His Peace.

Grow in spiritual maturity, within. That is the Kingdom of Yahweh.

WE NOW HAVE TWO CHOICES:

1. Continue to focus on assent to a creed and the Mithraic embellishments that made a man-Elohim of Brother Yeshua and created a Mithraic, ritualistic, controlling church. That over the centuries, persecuted and murdered over fifty million true Seventh Day Sabbath Keepers.

Read Revelation 18:2-4 in your own Bible especially verse 4.

2. Go back to Brother Yeshua's teachings and example, so we grow spiritually ourselves and we help humankind to grow into the Kingdom of Elohim, as Brother Yeshua envisioned.

Keep Yahweh's Sabbaths. That is Our Sign of belonging to Yahweh.

It sets us apart and the world does not like it.

Say Shema every day: Hear OH! Israel, Yahweh our Elohim is One and is the only Elohim.

I also say: Hear, OH! Israel, Yahweh our Elohim, is the Only Self Existent One.

I find that powerfully meaningful in rejecting all false gods and idols.

Pre-Sabbath: Wash our bodies as a symbolic sign of spiritual circumcision (keeping Torah, commandments), that's what those pools of water were for at entrances to ancient synagogues.

Keep His original scriptural truths, The Ten Commandments are you keeping them as instructed (what weekly Sabbath day do you keep? There is only one seventh day Sabbath), Read Leviticus 23? even if it means personal sacrifice,

Which will it be? Your physical life will be at risk and uncomfortable if you follow Yeshua's instruction to Love Yahweh your God with all your heart and with all your soul and with all your mind and with all your strength.'

But your Eternal Life will be secure.

About the
Author

Ernie Hasler started as an apprentice engineer in Bishopton, Scotland. He retired as a health and safety advisor after more than a half century of work on some big jobs.

He became active in the trade union and saw many improvements in health and safety during his time.

In his spare time, he ran a small charity Plant Tree Save Planet starting women's tree nurseries in poor countries, mostly funded by himself and his two sisters, however, he closed it when due to poor health and age he could not effectively check out recipients. He continues to fund tree planting through Trees for the Future and in 2016 funded the planting of 20,400 seedlings and continues to do so, year on year.

He has been a voluntary trustee with Emmaus Glasgow helping take it from an aspirational concept to a functioning community of up to twenty-seven previously homeless people, Emmaus Glasgow now also match his tree planting funding.

A far better policy would be to dig strong defensive positions all over the Highlands and make Scotland hard to invade.

Photo of Hasler steering friends boat past the lair of the nuclear monster's base on the River Clyde.